A PEOPLE APART

A PEOPLE APART

BY KATHLEEN KENNA

PHOTOGRAPHS BY ANDREW STAWICKI

HOUGHTON MIFFLIN COMPANY · BOSTON / NEW YORK 1995

For information about this and other Houghton Mifflin trade and reference
books and multimedia products, visit The Bookstore at Houghton Mifflin
on the World Wide Web at (http://www.hmco.com/trade/).

Manufactured in the United States of America

Book design by David Saylor
The text of this book is set in 14-point Simoncini Garamond.
The illustrations are black-and-white photographs reproduced as halftones.

HOR   10   9   8   7   6   5   4   3   2   1

LIBRARY OF CONGRESS CATALOGING-IN-PUBLICATION DATA
Kenna, Kathleen.
A people apart / by Kathleen Kenna ; photographs by Andrew Stawicki.
p. cm.   ISBN 0-395-67344-5
1. Old Order Mennonites—Juvenile literature. I. Stawicki, Andrew. II. Title.
BX8129.O43K46   1995
289.7'3—dc20   94-18545   CIP   AC

FRONTISPIECE: *A father and his sons going home from Sunday religious services*

For the congregation of the Hagerman Mennonite Church, with love and gratitude

—*Kathleen Kenna*

For the Mennonite people: may their simple lifestyle not be forgotten; may their traditions continue forever.

—*Andrew Stawicki*

Girls playing
on a buggy
at a farm auction

CONTENTS

Some Mennonites still farm their land with horse-drawn equipment.

The Mennonites

IN RURAL AREAS of North America, Old Order Mennonite families live without modern conveniences. In the fields, men harvest crops by hand and with horse-drawn equipment. Women wearing turn-of-the-century clothes cook on wood-burning stoves. Children studying in one-room schoolhouses dress almost like their parents, the boys in dark pants with suspenders, the girls in long dresses and aprons, their bonnets tied primly under their chins.

To outsiders, the Mennonites' way of life can seem uncomplicated as well as old-fashioned, but Mennonites have had to struggle to live as they do. During the past two centuries, Mennonites in the United States and Canada have been misunderstood, mistreated, and even put into prison because of their religious beliefs. Their ancestors in Europe were murdered for these same ideals.

In the 1500s, the Mennonites' ancestors called themselves Anabaptists—the "re-baptized." At that time only babies were baptized, but a priest named Ulrich

Zwingli and his supporters believed that adults should first learn what it means to be Christian, and then decide if they want to be baptized. On January 21, 1525, one of Zwingli's followers broke the law by conducting the first baptism of adults.

These baptisms were a challenge to the church and government, and European leaders ordered the Anabaptists killed. Five months after those first baptisms, an Anabaptist was executed. Many others were driven from their homes and had their possessions taken from them.

Anabaptists fled across Europe in search of religious freedom. Hiding in caves and on mountains, they traveled to any country that offered safety. Many settled in the Netherlands. There, in 1536, a Catholic priest named Menno Simons went into hiding with the Anabaptists. A year later, he was rebaptized and ordained as an Anabaptist leader. Menno Simons was so loved by his followers that they adopted his name: They called themselves Mennists or Mennonists and, later, Mennonites. Simons taught Anabaptism in secret. It was against the law even to be associated with him—one man was put to death just for letting Simons stay in his home.

Mennonite children are still told the story of Dirk Willems, who died demonstrating the Anabaptists' ideals of pacifism (peacefulness) and care of others. Anabaptist hunters were chasing him across a frozen river when one of them fell through the thin ice. Willems ran back and rescued the man, who immediately arrested him. This act of mercy cost Dirk Willems his life: He was burned at the stake in 1569. During the 1600s and 1700s, many Anabaptists were fined, imprisoned, tortured, and killed for refusing to give up their religion.

Through the years, the Mennonites have settled in many places around the

The Mennonites have marked graves with simple white headstones since they first came to North America.

world, including Asia, Africa, Australia, and Latin America. Some Mennonites live in traditional "Old Order" communities in the countryside. Others are "progressives," leading more modern lives in cities. But wherever they are, they try to live simply and humbly. Sometimes congregations divide when they disagree about which parts of modern life they will accept. The Amish began in this way. In 1693, a Swiss Mennonite bishop named Jacob Ammann broke away from the other Anabaptists because he thought they were becoming too modern. Many of his rules, such as using hooks and eyes instead of buttons, are still followed by Old Order Amish.

Mennonites do not usually allow their pictures to be taken, because they believe that pride is a sin. They do not have family photograph albums or carry photographs of their children. That would be considered showing off. Many of the people in this book had never been photographed. Some had never even spoken with anyone who was not a Mennonite, because they believe that in order to preserve their traditions, they should stay separate from people who are not Mennonites. But as they came to trust us, members of several Old Order congregations spoke about their lives and welcomed us into their homes and meetinghouse. They agreed to be photographed and to speak with us about their lives because they want readers to understand how Mennonites live.

Old Order children are not used to being photographed or to having visitors come to their school.

Every Sunday morning this Old Order meetinghouse is surrounded by buggies.

At the Meetinghouse

THE CLATTER OF carriage wheels and the rhythmic *clop* of horses' hoofs are the only sounds breaking the silence of a Sunday morning. Hundreds of people dressed in black clothes sweep by in dark buggies, raising spirals of dust along the dirt roads. Some have traveled for more than an hour, rattling along back roads flanked by trim farmhouses and by vast fields of haystacks and corn.

As dozens of buggies come together from different directions, they create an odd traffic jam of animals and people. A few horses snort; a baby cries from beneath a wool blanket; the long lines of gleaming black buggies stop at a flashing signal. The traffic light is the only sign that the modern world exists.

The buggies clatter along a paved road now, wheels whirling more rapidly, until they reach a low building standing in the middle of open farmland. This white clapboard building is the meetinghouse. It is the center of Old Order Mennonite life and an example of the simplicity that marks everything that is Mennonite.

The arrival of so many people and horses and buggies is surprisingly quiet. There are no loud greetings or laughter, only an occasional nod or polite murmur as people climb out of their buggies or arrive on foot. The women and girls go to one side of the meetinghouse to wait for services to begin. Their faces are hidden by stiff-brimmed black bonnets tied under their chins. Gathered at the other side of the meetinghouse are the men and boys, who wear dark, simply cut suits and plain black coats. The only flash of color among the black clothing is the pretty blue of the babies' blankets and the children's hand-knit mittens and scarves.

One little girl helps her father put a blanket over their horse to keep him warm, then skips off to meet her friends. The children chatter happily, but quietly. Although they have not seen one another for a week, they must be well behaved and not make noise or run around. Obedience—to God, parents, and Old Order traditions—is a lesson the children learn at home, school, and church.

Girls, young women, older women, boys, and men enter the meetinghouse separately, through five doors. Inside, there is one cloakroom for males and another for females. In their cloakroom, women and girls hang their coats, scarves, and bonnets on pegs. Mothers remove their babies' blankets and talk quietly among themselves. Unmarried women and girls gather at the back of the room to discuss the week's activities. The little girls line up before they enter the main room, where services will be held.

As they wait, a few of the girls play with their long braids. Like some other religions, Old Order Mennonites believe that women should not look like men, so all the women have long hair. Older girls and women wear their hair pinned in buns

*Old Order meetinghouses have separate entrances
for boys, girls, young women, older women, and men.*

and covered by delicate handmade white prayer caps. Women cover their heads as a sign of modesty and respect for God. Mennonites differ in their rules about the caps, but the women of this congregation wear their caps all day. Even while they sleep, many Old Order women wear a kerchief over their hair.

Everyone is dressed very simply. The little girls wear cotton dresses printed with pastel-colored patterns. Their mothers and the other women wear similar dresses in darker colors, mostly blue or black. No one wears jewelry, not even a watch or a wedding ring. The men and boys are dressed plainly too. Each congregation sets its own dress code—some allow men to wear ties, while others require jackets that fit snugly at the neck—but all the members of one congregation follow the same rules. Wearing old-fashioned clothes is one of the ways that the Old Order separates itself from the modern world.

The Mennonites' meetinghouse has no stained-glass windows, statues, or paintings. Like many Old Order homes, it does not have electricity or indoor plumbing. There is a wood-burning stove for heat, and the only light is the sunlight that filters through the windows. There are no sinks or flush toilets in the bathrooms, only wooden privies—indoors for women, outdoors for men.

As the members of the congregation enter the main room of the meetinghouse, they seat themselves in a U-shape around the pulpit. Men sit on one side, women on the other. This arrangement of people around the leaders' platform reflects the community's concern for each of its members. Older people sit close to the platform where they can see and hear more easily. Mothers with babies sit near the

All meetinghouses are single rooms with plain pine benches and no decorations. The metal hooks above the benches are for the men's hats. A deacon has the meetinghouse to himself before the congregation arrives.

exits so they can leave to feed an infant or to quiet one who is crying. Teens and unmarried young people sit in the back. The central front benches are for the younger children. They sit in front of their mothers and older brothers and sisters who sometimes whisper warnings about fidgeting. There is no separate Sunday school for the children.

All the ministers, bishops, and deacons who sit on the platform are men. The Old Order follows the passage from the New Testament that says women should keep silent in church.

After the deacons read from the New Testament, the ministers deliver sermons about obedience, discipline, and repentance. The service reinforces the principles by which Mennonites try to live each day. The sermons and readings remind members of the congregation to live simply, humbly, and in peace. They must not show off, and they are not allowed to fight—not even in self-defense or in a war.

Mennonite ministers are not paid for their work. Most are full-time farmers. And ministers do not go to Bible college or attend special classes. Instead, they are chosen "by lot." Male elders recommend congregation members who they believe would make good ministers. Then these men attend a meeting where each receives a book. One book contains a slip of paper, and the man who is given that book is believed to have been chosen by God to be a minister. Deacons and bishops are chosen in the same way.

Whether they live in Pennsylvania or Ontario, Canada, the ministers deliver their sermons in the form of German called Pennsylvania German. (It is sometimes called Pennsylvania Dutch because the German word for "German" is *Deutsch*.)

If there are visitors who do not understand that language, ministers will speak English, but Old Order Mennonites use German at home and among themselves. The language dates to the 1600s, when thousands of Mennonites left Germany and other countries in Europe and settled in Pennsylvania. Speaking German is another way the community keeps itself separate.

The German hymns they sing are hundreds of years old and are sung without the accompaniment of musical instruments. Old Order Mennonites believe a piano or organ would distract people from the words of the hymns. And there is no choir: Everyone is encouraged to sing and no one is singled out as special.

The service is several hours long and as it ends, some of the children are obviously excited to be going back outside. Everyone lines up to leave, the boys elbowing and nudging each other as they press toward the exits. Their fathers leave by another door to ready the horses for the journey home, and the girls join their mothers in the cloakrooms. Some of the boys and young men joke around outside, but there are only murmurs of conversation from the women and girls as they wait for their fathers, husbands, or brothers to arrive with the horses and buggies.

On Sunday, after services, Mennonites visit friends and relatives.

TWO

Sundays

IN FARMING COMMUNITIES, where people work six days a week from dawn until after dusk, a day of rest is precious. Sunday offers time away from everyday chores—time to read the Bible with the family, to reflect on the morning's sermon, and to relax with friends. For hundreds of years, Sunday has been the day that Mennonites visit each other. They may travel many hours by horse and buggy to see friends or relatives. No invitations are offered and none is expected, so no one knows how many visitors to expect. It is even possible that a family might set out to visit friends and find no one home when they arrive.

When Stanley Martin, who is one of the ministers, and his family return home to their farm, they are greeted by the fragrance of the homemade bread and other foods they left warming in the oven of the big wood-fire cookstove. Stanley goes out to the barn to feed the animals—some work cannot stop even on Sundays. The oldest child, four-year-old Dorcas, is only a little taller than the dining table, but she helps her mother, Elsie, set out dishes and silverware. Farm children learn at an early age to help with the chores. Elsie Martin must prepare a large meal since she does not know how many people will visit, but much of the food has been cooked ahead of time. On Saturday, many women cook for Sunday, clean the house thoroughly, and do the week's baking.

"We always have lots of food," Elsie says. "We prepare for many, but if only a few or no one comes, we will have lots of leftovers." A roast beef and several casseroles are cooking in the oven. The cupboards are filled with vegetables and fruits preserved in glass jars. Most families in the community have well-stocked pantries. Some also have root cellars that were dug out of the ground and made

Many Old Order Mennonite women cook on wood-burning stoves.

into cupboards. Root vegetables like potatoes, carrots, and turnips will remain fresh there all winter, kept cool but protected from freezing.

As in many farmhouses, there is no dining room. The big dining table is in the middle of the kitchen, so that dishes and food can easily be carried back and forth. Company has arrived and the women soon fill the table with food typical of an Old Order household: homemade sausages, scalloped potatoes, farm-smoked ham, green beans, home-canned chutney and corn relish, several salads, and home-baked bread. In some more modern Mennonite homes in cities, the meal after church is served cold, to reduce the amount of work, and it is often very plain, as a reminder of the many people in the world who do not have enough food. But in the country, the Old Order's big meals are a chance to share farm produce—meat from the family's animals, vegetables from their garden, fruit from their orchard—and to give thanks for the earth's bounty.

Often the men will talk in the parlor while the women work together in the kitchen. Outsiders sometimes criticize old-fashioned Mennonites for ignoring women's rights, but one Old Order woman says, "I wouldn't want to live another way. This is the way we were brought up, and we believe the Bible when it says men are the head of the household." Farm women have worked alongside men in the fields and barns since the days of the early settlers. The women often co-own the farms with their husbands, do some of the banking, and help make major decisions affecting their families, including the sale of land. Their husbands share in taking care of the children—although the women say that changing a baby's diapers is the one thing most men will not do.

When everyone comes to the table, they bow their heads in silent prayer and give thanks. During the meal, their conversation includes several jokes about Mennonites gaining weight from eating so much homemade food. Elsie laughs especially hard, because she has made several desserts, including a trifle made of cake and fruit topped with whipped cream. After the meal, there is another silent prayer. Daily dinners are not usually as large as Sunday dinners, but the ritual of giving thanks begins and ends every Old Order meal.

When the midday meal is over, and guests have gone home, young people—or whole families—sometimes get together for a baseball game. Everyone still wears Sunday clothes. At other times of the year, the children gather at ponds, where they skate in winter and swim in summer. The boys may wear shorts or bathing suits, but the girls swim in their long dresses. Boys and girls do not swim together, because they are not supposed to see each other partially dressed.

On Sunday night after dinner, children may play board games, but there are no televisions, radios, or computers—the Mennonites believe such things will distract them from what is important and expose them to influences from the outside world. Sunday night is also a time for families to read aloud. They own few books or magazines, partly because farm work leaves little leisure time and partly because Mennonites object to the obscene language and descriptions of violence found in many publications. In addition to reading the Bible, they enjoy rural newspapers, as well as Mennonite papers and journals. Sometimes parents read Bible stories to their children after they have tucked them in for the night. Bedtime comes early for many families: They will wake at dawn on Monday morning to begin work.

Only the most
necessary farm
chores and house
work are done on
Sundays, because
the Bible says that
people should rest
on the Sabbath.
Baseball is one
Sunday pastime;
swimming is
another.

When crops are harvested by hand, everyone on an Old Order farm must help. The men use pitchforks to toss hay onto wagons, and the children help drive the horses.

THREE

Mennonites at Work

MOST OLD ORDER Mennonites work as their great-grandparents did, on family farms. Their daily lives are shaped by hard work that changes with the seasons. Seeds are planted in the spring. Crops are tended in the early summer and harvested in the late summer and fall. Fall is also the time when women preserve food for their families, and men store feed for the livestock. Crops are sold, and animals may be sent to market. Winter allows more leisure time, but work on a farm is constant: Animals require year-round attention, and houses and barns need repairs or maintenance. In all seasons, family members must be fed and clothed.

Although not all Old Order Mennonites are farmers, the range of work they do is not wide. In Stanley Martin's community, there is a 76-year-old buggy-maker who builds plain buggies for Old Order families and fancy carriages for collectors and businesses around the world. Two cousins make wooden parts for buggies. An Old Order blacksmith shoes horses and makes tools, but the veterinarian is not a

Mennonite. One family runs a small dry-goods shop from their basement because the father was injured in a farming accident and can no longer farm. They sell fabric, shoes, and housewares. At another house, a woman makes hats, supplying most of the local women with their bonnets. Although most food is grown, preserved, and cooked at home, some groceries and household supplies are bought at non-Mennonite stores nearby. For many of their other needs, the Mennonites must travel farther out of the community.

Whether they are farmers caring for the soil, teachers watching over children in classrooms, or housewives tending their families, Old Order Mennonites see their work as a type of stewardship—of carefully nurturing what has been entrusted to them and making sure it thrives.

All over the world, Mennonites are known as caretakers of the soil. They regard the earth with reverence. Their love of the land is more than an appreciation of nature and an enjoyment of the rewards of their labor. It springs from their history of persecution. Land becomes especially precious to people whose ancestors were banished from their homes and who fled from country to country. They care for the land to support their families and try to preserve it for their children.

Long before most people were concerned about pollution and other abuses of natural resources, Mennonites used farming methods that did not harm the environment. They do not use chemicals to kill insects or weeds. The horse-drawn plows still used by some Mennonites do not pollute the air or use fossil fuel.

The Old Order Mennonites say that farming and hard work cement family bonds, which they believe are lacking in the outside world. On a farm, parents and

Edwin Martin's buggy-making and -repairing business has become so successful that he gets orders from as far away as South America.

In an Old Order home that has no electricity, kerosene lamps give this woman the light she needs for hooking a rug—although more lights were used to take this photograph.

children can work side by side. When Onias and Mary Metzger go to their barn to milk the cows every evening, all of their children tag along. The littlest ones sit on a bench and watch, but nine-year-old Shirley and her younger brothers spray iodine on the cows' udders to help prevent infection, and help untangle some of the milking machinery.

As Mennonite children get older, they do more and more work. When the boys are old enough, they use big draft horses or tractors to plow fields and harvest crops. Girls help their mothers in the house and barn. Shirley Metzger already shares some of the daily cooking and housecleaning with her mother, and often watches the five smaller children.

Work and leisure may sometimes be the same on an Old Order farm. When the daily chores of cleaning house and preparing meals are done, many Mennonite women relax by sewing their own dresses and aprons. Clothing that is too difficult or would take too long to make at home, such as underwear, socks, and shoes, is purchased from a Mennonite store. Some women also make rugs.

Mennonite women are famous for their beautiful quilts. Some of the quilts are used by the families; others are sold at an annual auction that raises money for charity. Making the tiny even stitches may seem like hard work, but many of the women enjoy quilting. They meet at each other's homes regularly to sew around a big square quilting frame, working and socializing at the same time. At home, after a mother finishes her daily tasks, quilting offers some quiet time with her daughters, while she teaches them how to sew something that is both pretty and practical. Sewing together is work and play at the same time.

Mennonite congregations have a "dress code" and avoid many—but not all—modern conveniences.
This woman and her family are returning from a trip to town to buy a newspaper.

FOUR

"To Be in the World But Not of the World"

AT FIRST GLANCE, an Old Order farm looks like any farm. One difference is that usually a buggy is parked outside the garage, instead of a car. Inside the house, although people may have some antiques handed down from generation to generation, the furniture is mostly ordinary and plain. There is little decoration—a calendar with country scenes is often the only picture on the walls. But if we look closely, there is another difference: Often there are no power lines leading to the house, because many Old Order Mennonites refuse to have electricity.

Electricity, cars, and telephones belong to the modern world—a world offering temptations that may lure people away from their traditions. Old Order Mennonites are taught to be "in the world, but not of the world," which means they try to avoid being distracted by the modern world's emphasis on money, possessions, and pride in one's accomplishments. Telephones, cars, radios, and televisions are part of that world and also make it easier to reach.

Old Order families who have telephones use them only for business purposes, like making appointments to see a doctor or arranging to have the horse fitted with shoes. Some construct little sheds at the end of their driveways where a telephone is available for emergencies. But a telephone is not used for chatting with friends.

Many Old Order farms are a mixture of the modern and the traditional. On one farm there is electricity but no telephone. There is a horse and buggy instead of a car. There is a power lawn mower but no dishwasher. Each congregation makes its own rules about such things, and members must live by those rules.

Sometimes people disagree with their congregation's rules. Onias Metzger decided he needed a telephone to manage his farming business: "I asked the bishop why [phones are banned] and he said it's a tradition. The church just thought it wasn't needed. The bishop said we could be excommunicated. I say, my Bible is the same Bible as theirs. My Bible doesn't tell me if I should drive a car or if I should have a telephone. What's the difference if I have a telephone in my home or I use my neighbor's?" After the Metzgers and several other families installed telephones in their homes, they were asked to leave the congregation. If they had removed the phones and apologized, they would have been allowed to stay. But Onias said he "couldn't see what was wrong with it," so his family was expelled.

For centuries, expulsion (which is also called excommunication) has been a way of enforcing the rules that hold a community together. Common reasons for excommunication are divorce, alcoholism, or dishonesty. But congregations try to avoid expelling anyone. They vote for excommunication only after offering counseling, prayers, and forgiveness.

Onias Metzger is looking at the first photograph of himself that he has ever seen. His wife, Mary, prefers not to look, since Old Order tradition says that having photographs of oneself is a sign of pride.

Excommunication often includes a practice called banning or shunning, which means that members who are forced to leave the congregation are no longer accepted in the community, even socially. Friends and relatives may not speak to people who have been banned. But someone who has been excommunicated is welcomed back if the congregation agrees that the person is willing to follow community rules in the future.

Families that are excommunicated usually join other congregations or establish a new one. Generally, it is only an individual, like a teenager who has been in trouble with the police or an alcoholic man no longer living with his family, who will leave the Mennonites altogether.

The Metzgers' new congregation allows cars as well as telephones, and after the birth of his sixth child Onias bought a black van. The new congregation that Onias and his family belong to is known as "black car" Old Order. It is sometimes called "black bumper," because the chrome on a new car will be removed or painted black. This congregation allows trucks, vans, and cars, but only black ones, so that members are not tempted to show them off. Onias removed the van's radio. Although this congregation follows different rules from his old one, Onias emphasizes that he is still an Old Order Mennonite.

Members of congregations like Onias's argue that telephones and cars have become necessary as the world has changed. Seeing a doctor or even going to the hardware store requires traveling a greater distance than it did in the past. But others say the ban on cars and phones is necessary to ensure that Old Order customs do not disappear little by little.

Yet, even in more conservative congregations, traditions change. Making a farm profitable today requires more land, more labor, and more machinery than it did in the early 1700s, when Mennonites first began farming in North America. Some older farmers still use huge Clydesdale or other draft horses instead of tractors, but many farmers say tractors and other machinery are necessary if Mennonites are to continue the tradition of preserving the land for their children.

In spite of the Mennonites' skill, farms sometimes fail. Often this means that a family will be forced to leave the land that it has owned for generations and that the farm and the family's possessions will be sold at an auction. Or, an auction may be held because an elderly man has died and there is no one to take over his farm. A farm auction is considered such an important community event that sometimes

LEFT: *At an auction, men and boys inspect the hand-stitched leather upholstery of a buggy that is for sale.*

BELOW: *Farmers wait to bid on a woodstove.*

the children are dismissed early from school so they can attend. Although the occasion is a sad one, it is also a gathering that allows people to socialize and to buy things they need.

Old Order Mennonites must remain true to their traditions while deciding what parts of the modern world to accept. "It's the material things that divide us," one farmer says. "We all have disagreements about modernism. 'If only I could have this; if only I could have that.'" But being an Old Order Mennonite means living differently than most people live. It means giving up many of the machines that make work easier. It also means looking different from other people.

As a young girl, Elsie Martin went to a public school with many non-Mennonite children and she wished her church allowed other kinds of clothing. "Oh, sure, sometimes I wished I could wear a brighter color or have a larger print on my dresses, but it didn't really matter. It didn't stop us from being friends," she says.

Young girls sometimes wish they could wear pants, Elsie says. "I have never worn trousers, except to play act at home when I was a little girl," she adds. "Oh, you would never wear them in public." Some Old Order parents do not allow their daughters to put on pants even for playing dress-up.

By following strict rules about their clothing, Old Order Mennonites show that the group is more important than the individual. They wear simple, plain clothing to show that they are not proud about their appearance. They do not spend time or money following the latest fashions. Like uniforms at some schools, Old Order dress is a sign of equality: Rich and poor dress alike. And like others who wear a particular costume as part of their heritage, Old Order Mennonites dress alike to

Most people in this community buy their inexpensive running shoes from the same Mennonite-owned store.

show membership in a group that shares the same ideals. Their clothing is a constant reminder to outsiders and to themselves of their values.

When Old Order families visit neighboring towns and cities, they sometimes find themselves stared at or mocked. "We just hope that people see beyond our clothes, that they realize there's more to us than our different way of dressing," one woman says. "I hope they see the Christianity in us."

With their old-fashioned clothes and long braids, these girls do not look much different from the children who went to country schools 100 years ago, except for their lunch boxes. Plastic lunch boxes are practical and simple, so the Old Order sees no reason to not to use them.

FIVE

Old Order Schools

FOR MORE THAN 200 years, the Mennonites have tried to operate their own schools. It has been a long struggle.

One of the most dramatic battles over education took place in western Canada during the 1920s, after World War I. People in Canada and the United States who spoke German were harassed during the war years, because Germany was one of the countries Canada and the United States were fighting against. Public anger was especially fierce toward the Mennonites and Amish, who refused to serve in the military. In the United States, pacifists' homes were painted yellow. Their ministers were tarred and feathered. Children were sometimes called traitors because their fathers and older brothers would not go to war.

In Canada, Mennonites were forbidden to speak German in their schools. They were required to send their children to schools that taught the government-approved lessons. But in the province of Manitoba, the classrooms sat empty. The

Mennonites kept their children at home, and they were fined. Some refused to pay the fines and were put in jail. Some, too poor to pay, had their farms taken from them and sold at auctions. Many eventually moved. Between 1922 and 1927, 7,000 Mennonites left Canada for Mexico and Paraguay.

Similar arguments have flared in other communities. In the United States, Amish parents who refused to send their children to public schools were arrested, fined, and sent to jail. Then, in 1972, the United States Supreme Court ruled that the Amish should be allowed to run their own school system because it suits their way of life and religious beliefs. The judges said, "a way of life that is odd or even erratic but interferes with no rights or interests of others is not to be condemned because it is different." This ruling protects Amish and Mennonite schools.

Most Old Order Mennonite schools are one- or two-room buildings that were constructed by members of the congregation. Often the schools have outhouses instead of indoor toilets. Some schools are still heated by woodstoves and lit by kerosene lamps. Many have old-fashioned wooden desks with holes in the tops for inkwells, although students now use ballpoint pens.

About halfway between the Martin and Metzger farms stands a small schoolhouse that was a public school until it was bought by an Old Order congregation in 1967. It has electricity. The principal says some students are so fascinated by the electric lights that they spend their first few days of school flicking the light switches on and off.

Several grades study in one room, just as they did in most rural schools until the middle of this century. In the junior class, the first to third graders are taught by

Lydia Martin. In the senior class, next door, the fourth to eighth graders are taught by the principal, Amsey Martin. (They are not related to Stanley and Elsie Martin or to each other; Martin is a common name in this community.)

The pictures that almost completely cover the walls show that this is a country school. The senior class has drawn pictures of cows to learn the different breeds raised in their community. The younger children have cut out tractors and patchwork quilt designs. The junior class also colors pictures of more exotic animals, like elephants, to learn the letters of the alphabet. But they do not take their pictures home—that would be showing off.

Amsey Martin calls everyone into the schoolhouse by ringing the brass bell on the roof. The school day begins with the Lord's Prayer and with hymns. Hymns are also sung at the close of morning classes and at the end of the day. Mr. Martin lets the students pick their favorites. Then the children are invited to share community news with their classmates.

Once classes begin, the room is very quiet. The children are solemn, rarely smiling or even looking at each other. While they do written exercises, the only sound is the occasional *click-click-click* of a horse and buggy going along the road outside. Students raise their hands to ask questions or to respond to their teacher. Speaking out of turn or whispering to classmates is not allowed.

Anyone who disobeys is scolded immediately. Sometimes students will not be allowed to go outside at recess or lunchtime if they misbehave. Children who ignore the teacher's warnings are slapped on the palms of their hands with a rubber strap. Many public school districts have banned the strap, but Old Order

parents and teachers believe it is a good way to teach the importance of obedience.

With many grades in each room, there is good reason for the students to be quiet. While the seventh graders read silently, Mr. Martin asks the other students to spell the words he reads aloud. He spreads four spelling texts out across his desk, calling out words for each grade. During the school day, Mr. Martin will repeat this juggling of four or five books for other subjects.

The school uses 50-year-old textbooks from the public school system. Most current books used in public schools are unacceptable to the Old Order, because the Mennonites find the language crude or the subjects unsuitable for their children. Many Old Order teachers write and design their own texts. These homemade books are typewritten and hand bound, and contain information about farm and Mennonite life. Although there are no new books on the school's library shelves, the collection includes *The Black Stallion, Robinson Crusoe, Heidi, Little Women,* and many volumes of *The Bobbsey Twins* series.

In Old Order schools, students study the same subjects as public school students do—English, geography, math, spelling, health studies, science, and history—but some of the material included in their lessons may be different. There is no sex education taught in the health class, for example, and history classes include the study of the Mennonites from the 1500s to the present. A typical notebook of a seventh grader includes information on nuclear energy, environmental issues like dwindling schools of codfish in the Atlantic Ocean, and the importance of fruit farming in eastern North America.

The senior classroom, for fourth to eighth graders, is very quiet,
even when all the grades are doing different work. Mr. Martin
was not at school the day this picture was taken.

Old Order students in this school study the Bible for only a half hour each week. "We believe in teaching manners and kindness and honesty—it's religion at work," says Mr. Martin. "We don't need to teach a whole lot of religion. Religion is part of our everyday lives." The school reinforces principles like the Mennonites' belief in not fighting, he explains. "It may start in the sandbox. If someone hits you, you're not allowed to hit back."

Recesses are short—15 minutes in the morning and 15 in the afternoon. During their hour-long lunch break, the children eat the sandwiches and fruit they have brought from home, and dash outdoors as soon as they can.

Soccer is popular, but baseball is the favorite game, and students bring their gloves to school even before the snow has melted completely. Boys, girls, and teachers play together, the girls running in their long skirts with braids flying out behind them. There is very little cheering, even for home runs, and there are no shouts of "Pick me! Pick me!" when teams are chosen. The children do not boast about winning or make fun of the losers. Sometimes they do not keep score at all. Even competitive sports are played in a way that does not encourage pride.

In winter, the children skate and play hockey on frozen ponds or on a flooded patch of schoolyard. In warmer weather, the older students play tag, baseball, or soccer; the younger ones play with jump ropes or on swings and seesaws. Their farms are far apart, so school is the main place to see friends.

ONE AFTERNOON, members of the senior class talked about the differences between Mennonites and non-Mennonites. The students say they doubt that

Sometimes even the teacher joins the baseball game.

others their age would want to exchange their modern lives for Old Order ways.

"They probably wouldn't want to live without TV or radio," says 13-year-old Clarence. But he wouldn't want to give up his way of life either. He enjoys "working in the fields, driving a baler and cultivator." The others agree they do not want televisions, partly because their parents would not approve and partly because, "you would just be sitting around all the time." Harvey prefers to ride horses or go fishing. Beverly would not want a television because "You're apt to see too many murders."

Most of the students have seen televisions in stores, but have never watched a whole program. One boy did not recognize a television when his family made a recent trip to a hardware store. "Sometimes I'm surprised by how little our children know [about the outside world]," Mr. Martin says. "Most don't have a yearning for these modern things because they haven't encountered them."

When the members of the senior class were asked what they want to be when they leave school, they all gave the same answer: The boys want to be farmers, and the girls want to be homemakers. They do not want to go to college, even to become doctors or veterinarians who could work in their community. The Old Order believes that education beyond the eighth grade is unnecessary. But the school does prepare students for living and working in their community. As future farmers, they learn about weather patterns, animal care, and soil conditions. They are also given a solid knowledge of reading, writing, and mathematics.

Most young people do not question the rules set for them by the Old Order. It is the only world they know. Some teenagers do rebel and may leave the Old

Order to find work in factories or on farms. Many of them return, once they realize that the close-knit Mennonite community offers a safety and security they may not find in the modern world. The Old Order community promises young people a future that is much the same as their past—a circle of friends and family who follow the same traditions and are committed to the same ideals.

After they leave school, Old Order teenagers continue to learn farm work. Their families believe that more schooling tends to make people "worldly"—interested in the things of the world.

Teenagers on their way to visit friends

SIX

Young People

WHEN 14-YEAR-OLD Beverly leaves school at the end of the year, she will probably work on a farm until she marries. She may continue helping her parents or she may work on another Old Order farm, being paid room, board, and a small salary for doing housework, baby sitting, and helping with chores.

One reason governments allow Old Order teens to leave school early is that, like Beverly, they will continue to learn at home, through experience. Some get library books to continue studying subjects that interested them at school; others may take courses by mail, such as health care or bookkeeping.

Principal Amsey Martin studied accounting by mail, and now prepares income-tax forms for his neighbors. Like all Old Order teachers, he left school after eighth grade. To become a teacher, he had to be chosen by a school board of Old Order parents who checked his marks and interviewed him to see if his personality suited teaching. They also talked to farmers he had worked for as a teenager.

"I would love to go to a university because I have a questing mind," the principal says, "but I wouldn't go, because I think you become what you're exposed to in your environment. We stay in a closed society because we think the evil rubs off on you."

This belief in the evils of the outside world—drinking, smoking, sex before marriage, dishonesty, over-valuing material goods, pride—colors daily life in Old Order communities. Adults believe that children and teenagers can be easily influenced by modern ways and may be tempted to stray from the Old Order culture if they spend too much time with non-Mennonite friends. In their late teens or early twenties, young people decide if they want to be baptized, so this is an especially important time.

"We feel the teen years are a time when they should be under a parent's guidance all the time, working and not sitting in school," Stanley Martin says. "Physical work all day makes them tired and not so apt to give in to fleshly desires."

The Mennonites still use the old-fashioned term "courting" to describe dating. Before they begin courting, the man and woman often write to each other. The man sends the first letter and asks the woman if he can take her home from the young people's Sunday evening social gathering.

On Sunday nights the young people meet at a farmhouse after the evening meal to talk and sing religious songs. As they did at school, they sing without any musical accompaniment, in four-part harmony, the girls sitting on one side of the room, the boys on the other. After refreshments, everyone leaves, some young men on bicycles and others in buggies. When a couple is courting, the man escorts the woman to her home, where they may talk for a few hours. He will meet her parents, but usually the couple is trusted to sit in the parlor by themselves.

"Sometimes you'll write back and forth for a while to see if your ideals and views of life are matched," one woman explained. "And then, if the girl wants to go with him, he will take her home in his buggy. If it doesn't work out, then they'll break it off and people may not even know they were going together."

ABOUT ONE QUARTER of any Old Order population never marries. They often set up their own farms or households, sometimes with another unmarried friend or relative. Thomas Martin and Samuel Weber, 22-year-old cousins, share a home and business. After a hard week in the woodworking shop they operate from a big barn, they say they look forward to Sunday evening.

Thomas loves music and would like to have a radio, but he feels that if he bought one, he might then be tempted to buy a stereo. Soon he would adopt other modern ways: "I think it would be fun to drive a car too—it certainly would be handy—but our church says you can't. You have to have some guidelines to keep people together. This is an inheritance. It's not something you just give up."

Samuel and Thomas's belief in their community's traditions does not keep them from showing their independence. While most of their friends work on family farms and will someday take over their fathers' businesses, the cousins bought their own small company, where they bend and shape slender pieces of white ash to make the wooden spokes for wagon wheels and the shafts for buggies. Farmers buy these parts for repairs, and the local buggy-maker uses them rather than making his own. And the cousins have expanded their business. They now make hickory frames for snowshoes.

The two men say they do not regret leaving school in seventh grade. "We were taught to teach ourselves and that's all that's necessary," Samuel says. "You can get books at the library if you want to learn more." Thomas adds: "It's experience that teaches you best. What school should do is teach you to teach yourself. You go to school to learn how to reason, how to invent things for yourself."

The cousins are part of the large group of young people who want to maintain the old ways. Thomas and Samuel live in a farmhouse that has no electricity or refrigerator. They have a propane-fueled stove and a woodstove for cooking, and they heat their home with a wood-burning furnace. On their shelves is a combination of store-bought food, and preserves and home-canned food prepared by Thomas's mother. A box of Cheerios sits next to a jar of homemade applesauce.

They prefer to live by the light of kerosene lamps instead of having electricity. Thomas says, "Once you get it, it becomes too easy to hook up almost anything to it. It would be more of a burden than a luxury for us. I like the quiet. I don't want to hear the hum of a refrigerator or a freezer all the time. It's not that it's wrong, but [not having] it does help to keep you separate."

The cousins note that some young people follow Old Order rules even more carefully than their parents, living without electricity after having had it in their childhood homes. Others own cars and telephones. But Thomas and Samuel believe that Old Order people should not live like everyone else. They must live apart to preserve their way of life.

Thomas Martin (left) and Samuel Weber prefer kerosene lamps to electric lights.

The heavy sides of this new barn were built flat on the ground before they were pulled upright with ropes.

SEVEN

Barn Raising

ASIDE FROM THEIR commitment to peace, one of the most important Old Order beliefs is the importance of helping others. Mennonites raise money for the poor, dig wells in developing countries, and volunteer after natural disasters like hurricanes. But while Old Order Mennonites send money and sometimes workers to help the needy outside their community, they generally follow the old saying "charity begins at home."

The Mennonites accept no government welfare, social security, or pensions. Life insurance and property insurance are forbidden. Mennonites trust God to watch over them. To insure their lives would be a kind of gambling, and it would suggest that it is possible to put a price on life. It would also give strangers the responsibility for people who should be cared for by their family and community.

"We are our own insurance," says Onias Metzger. "If someone needs something, then I want to help him."

If sickness, injury, or other tragedy strikes an Old Order family, members of the congregation visit, prepare meals, take care of the children, and do farm work. If someone needs to be hospitalized, the congregation pays the bill.

Nowhere is this sense of community more remarkable than at a barn raising. Since an Old Order family has no insurance, a barn fire could ruin them financially. Instead, a crew of men, fed and watched over by the women, raise a barn from the ashes in little more than a day.

After one winter blaze, dozens of men and boys from ten different Mennonite congregations gathered at the farm. Construction was delayed by cold rain, and farmers delivered lumber and other supplies to the farm while they waited for the weather to clear. In kitchens across the countryside, Old Order women baked pies, bread, and other foods.

The call came early in the morning to Onias Metzger, who told some families by telephone. Families without phones were sent for by horse-and-buggy messenger. The men arrived, and the work continued from early morning until almost dark.

All day, the singsong of hammers and saws cracked the cold air, while men sweated over a mammoth wooden frame. A chief carpenter helped organize the work crews, directing the strongest builders to one corner, telling boys to haul nails to another. The barn skeleton took shape quickly from a tangle of men and tools and lumber. The carpenters, almost all farmers, fell into a natural rhythm, cooperating with few instructions and some friendly chatter. The younger men were so confident that they walked across high beams without safety harnesses.

As parts of the frame were ready to be raised, the men hoisted them into place without machinery, all shouting "Yo!" (Get ready) and "He!" (Push). Women watched from the farmhouse windows or stood near the barn site, waiting to offer refreshments. They spent hours preparing a huge meal for the lunch break. Tables were set up in the driving shed—a smaller barn used to store farm equipment—and the women served heaping plates of vegetables, meat, salads, and homemade bread. The women ate afterward, then washed and dried the dishes while the men completed as much of the outer shell as possible before darkness. The indoor work and the roof were finished another day by some of the same volunteers.

The congregation later shared the cost of the barn materials. "You're not compelled to pay a certain amount if you can't," says Edwin Martin, whose buggy-making shop is not far from the new barn. Figuring he has probably seen more barn raisings than most Old Order Mennonites, he adds, "You give what you can afford and you pay so that you are satisfied in your own mind that you have helped as best you can."

A man balances on the top of the new barn.

At a farm auction, women enjoy each other's company while men bid on the goods for sale. Old Order life continues to change, but Mennonite values endure.

EIGHT

The Future

AS THE MENNONITES near their five-hundredth anniversary, Old Order people say they cannot predict what the next century will bring to their communities. If the pace of change continues as it has in the past few decades, it seems likely that the Old Order in North America will keep splintering into new congregations over disagreements about which changes to accept.

But the international Mennonite church continues to grow. Of the 900,000 people in the world who call themselves Mennonites, only about 381,000 are in the United States and Canada. The church's members in Africa, Asia, Australia, and Latin America outnumber those in North America.

Through the centuries, the Mennonites have faced persecution—and even death—to remain true to their beliefs. Although communities may divide and some traditions may gradually change, the basic beliefs do not change. The Mennonites continue to try to live simply, humbly, and peacefully.

BIBLIOGRAPHY

Baerg, Anna. *The Diary of Anna Baerg*. Translated and edited by Gerald Peters. Winnipeg, Manitoba: CMBC Publications, 1987.

Dyck, Cornelius J., ed. *An Introduction to Mennonite History*. Scottdale, Penn.: Herald Press, 1981.

Epp, Frank H. *Mennonites in Canada, 1786–1920*. Toronto, Ontario: Macmillan of Canada, 1975.

——. *Mennonites in Canada, 1920–1940*. Toronto, Ontario: Macmillan of Canada, 1982.

Fretz, J. Winfield. *The Mennonites in Ontario*. Waterloo, Ontario: The Mennonite Historical Society of Ontario, 1982.

——. *The Waterloo Mennonites: A Community in Paradox*. Waterloo, Ontario: Wilfrid Laurier University Press, 1989.

Good, Merle and Phyllis. *20 Most Asked Questions About the Amish and Mennonites*. Lancaster, Penn.: Good Books, 1979.

Horst, Isaac R. *Separate and Peculiar*. Mount Forest, Ontario: Printed by the author, 1983.

Klaasen, Walter. *Anabaptism: Neither Catholic nor Protestant*. Waterloo, Ontario: Conrad Press, 1973.

Klaasen, Walter, ed. *Anabaptism Revisited*. Scottdale, Penn.: Herald Press, 1992.

Smith, C. Henry. *Smith's Story of the Mennonites*. Newton, Kans.: Faith and Life Press, 1981.

Van Braght, Thieleman. *Martyrs Mirror*. Scottdale, Penn.: Herald Press, 1950. (5th edition revised and enlarged by Cornelius Krahn)

Wengel, J. C. *What Mennonites Believe*. Scottdale, Penn.: Herald Press, 1991.